Kneeling Under the Lemon Tree

Kneeling Under the Lemon Tree

Poems by

Michele Lesko

Cover design: Shay Culligan

Cover art: Liza Head, Juniper Spring Photography, San Jose, CA.

ISBN: 978-1-949229-89-9

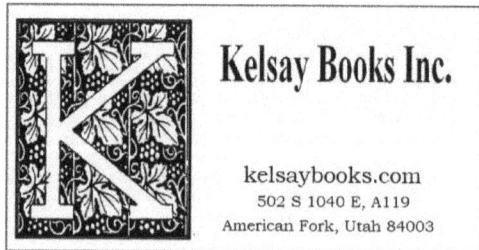

Kelsay Books Inc.

kelsaybooks.com
502 S 1040 E, A119
American Fork, Utah 84003

Dedication

This collection of poems is dedicated to my sons, Calvin, Jackson, and Carter, in appreciation for their determination in thinking about the world and its people in non-normative ways —and to their father for sharing with me in the creation of the best people I know. Our sons' lives were formed within the challenges, foibles, and successes that make a life. My experiences, independently and through connecting with the stories of others, are all in some way enfolded into the words on these pages.

Acknowledgments

"Initiation and Penance" first published in *Mannequin Envy;* "Twist the Oldest Love Story" & "A Circus Life" in *Soundzine;* "A Tufted Titmouse" in *The Literary Bohemian;* "Nine's the Devil His Own Self" in *The Southern California Review;* "September 11th Deliverance" in *Shitcreek Review;* "For Poetry" in *Salvage Magazine;* "Riding the Pretty Horse" and "His Hands" in *Soundzine;* "Queen Holle" in *Anon;* "Nothing But Laundry" in *Lily Literary Review;* "A Measure of Worth" in *The Yalobousha Review;* "Mother's Birthday in Paradise" in *Avatar Review.* "Interlude: Claridge's London" won a Reader's Choice Award in *The Pedestal Magazine.*

I also want to acknowledge that these poems are a journey of the mind, where information is gleaned from shared experience. Not many of the truly tragic events herein happened to me. "September 11th Deliverance," and its companion essay about the many ways we use the word 'fall,' came from Chief Editor Paul Stevens' request for a poem and essay about the 9/11 tragedy for *The Shitcreek Review.* I imagined the tragedy through the eyes of an abused child. I used my Catholic childhood combined with the childhood phase of magical thinking that affects all children. In that stage, one often believes one is at fault for collateral damage, when prayers are answered. I was blessed to have met Paul through the poetry community. He was an incredibly supportive poet friend. May he rest in peace.

Contents

Part 1:

Lemon Tree Roots

Mother's Birthday in Paradise: 1967

At home on Date Street mother slips into
a cotton shift after knocking mangoes from
our neighbor's tree. Their fruit and some

crayfish from our backyard stream make
up my supper. Walking to meet my father,
she pretties her hair with one moon-bright

Magnolia. On Waikiki he gives her jade
tears to hang from her ears. Twenty-seven
silver coins spent to match her years. Waiting

up for them, gut-rubbed by the raw desire
for food, I stare at the painted pig
that lay shattered on my bed. He broke it

for a jeweler's box instead of the market bag
promise of flesh after a season of rice. My
Dad's once-upon-a-time still keeps me
sleeping meat and potato dreams.

The Coffin and the Priest

We stand at the waist of her
casket. Our priest reveals nothing.

He celebrates. With Revelation he
enters my mother among the dead.

This man who saved my newborn
soul. His finger eased sacred chrism

down my temple. Eleven years passed
before this priest anointed me again

with his appetite for spirits. Father Tim
entered me among the living. His sweat

stained collar hovered above me. I itched
to color it. Red. After school no one came

for me except him. The apse curled
around us while he held me apart

from a flock whose parents were never late.
We stand before the altar, united in sorrow

with our open palms on the edge
of her polished box.

Left Wanting

Sister, I want our father in the worst way
wanting his body like a host from beyond
that grave you chose without knowing him.

I want him the way he wanted that six pound
lobster, who, he laughed, *must've lived forever*
before our want. We wanted it outside its shell

and inside of us, sweet and melting hot. I want
our father, you, *Dad,* not the hard, cold creature
            who appeared after your shell turned

from soft sand to sallow in the unsettled hours
after you left your body. There is a wanting
that demands we digest, subsume, the lost

flesh into our own. Like a cannibal wants
that failed fist of blood that signifies. I
want you inside of me. Embryo to every

thing that ever was. I want to liquefy pain,
harbor your broken body, ingest your liver
which, like that lobster's shrill, will emit
the perfectly pitched note of remembrance.

It's Over Now

It's over now, and I want to write
pretty words that speak adult
sentences
                drained of the life
sentence of tell-all-storying you.

But then I recall the little blue
Navion
              that flew
across the road the day I found out
you had flown away. Trees burst
into bloom like a community
      waving *you, you, you* on
              into the not here,

not now, never again. We once sat
on fresh grass with a baby between
us. I felt you knowing you'd never
know him.   And you cried.
A great sobbing not for you, for me
you said,   *You will be the only
              one who suffers.*

And so I did, naturally
            like a bird
a starling shoved off the topmost
limb. I was old, should have been
ready. Instead, I fell and continue
            to tumble
like a child untethered
            on a carnival ride.
            The road before me
unfurls in every direction. Like you

I travel to where I have not been
to curve around lakes   to stop
beneath an endless sky   to read
                planes taking their leave.

Who knew an act so   common
would leave me   more alone
than St. Clare who refused marriage
for solitude   in silence
                signs appear
to lead the way
                to the place
called home by you.   In this age
of ease   I long to crawl
out of this cave
where fire   casts shadows
                puppets dance, but
I do not want to speak.   I do not want
to flicker in false firelight.

Her Raging Body

I stare at you. New to me and this earth. I try
to relive *her* rage. Desperate, she kicked you
down a long run of stairs. I am almost able to

envision the fall. Her once young, often bruised
body released you & right quick shed its twisted
cord. Your blood letting her mind go on day one

she dropped you in dirt; okra meant for another
stew. You grow for me although I can't match her
dreaming you dead. Try as I might.   I study

beat up kids religiously. Punch-drunk pushed ones
who eat their hair inside dark closets. Unaware
you look up at me and grin! So I pry the edges

of my privileged vision, same way I peel the skin
from my ragged cuticles, craving the pain of pushing
you out this barren body because I need all
her *might of been* to simply be   your mother.

September 11th Deliverance

I am here. You are dead. And every year
someone sings your praise: Hero. I regret

that restless fall day, when scooped out
by your hand on my bee-stung chest, I prayed

the way you said I should—at bedtime. You said
let us pray. You began by making me kiss the tip

of the cross you wore. Kiss Christ's toe. A sacrament
you used to repent. It didn't help. I never saw Christ

and you were never a father, not a savior. And I was
not a child, born again as a novitiate. Ritual is a hook.

Reeling, I begged Him to deliver me; over and over
like a curse it worked. You jumped and died. Yet
other fathers kept falling, after you.

They Say I Must Invite Christ Inside Me

He just hangs there
unadorned   except for the nails
that make my palms itch.
                    I do not bleed
and cannot love him like the other Marys.

Magdalene with her body prepared to give
in, even leaving her womb open. His mother
                    a virgin like me, but whole
a woman ready to bear his body on her knees.

These women came to him through angels.

I have no choice. He comes to me all earthy
drops of vinegar and dirty   still.
                    Each day opens
with hymns and the lust that slithers across
                    my hips and down my thighs
like morning fog.

Maybe I will grow to love this sorrow.
                    No choice so,   maybe
I am one of the Marys.   I love him.   His body
                    is a gift they say.   No way
out of desire as I grow beneath his naked angles
each day   staring at the slender feet

that beg me.   . I turn thirteen and begin
to bleed   knowing he needs my hands
on his body.   He requires more praise

than any man   should.
His bleeding heart   a wound   we pray
we will learn to endure.   I have   no choice.

The Daughter

Imagine just one more Mary. Post-
pubescent goddess, engaged in a
ménage et trois of the spiritual bent.

It was a quiet town somewhere in Utah
where her body became a wound His
daughter poured from. Undone by her

miraculous ability to adapt, this one also
returned to the father but with a girlchild
bound to her breast. Celestial wife, she

joined the circus and taught herself to fly.
Too soon she will teach the girl to swing
and to drop with no fear of falling.

Twist the Oldest Love Story

Tell it across his table
on your first date. His face
will pale, when you slip him
your doubts about Mary

inviting God's desire to twist
her fate like the silk slip that slid
around your too thin waist
as you sidled up to his door.

Later, you choose to pass
on his offer of the apple
pie he serves. You feel less
American, downright un-

Godly under the weight of
him as he twists your skirt
off and takes his dessert
bent over the once clean cloth

of his sullied table. One date, one
twist of fate, and two virgins
convinced they slipped
into an unconventional desire.

The Perfect Swan Dive

Late June afternoons, her dad
wakes thirsty to drag her down
to the pool's high dive. She hides
her fear in a blue puddle. Black

sandpaper steps keep her from
slipping into the little girl world
where pleas let you back down
past hard boys who climb to smirk

their way to the top. There she is
on tiptoe, arms a cathedral, ribs
ladder through her Speedo. She
fills her lungs and holds her breath.

She is a girl poised on the thin lip
of a springboard, where she becomes
light and lets all her energy, tucked
away each day and labeled love, live
in the balls of her feet.

Initiation and Penance

The leaves beneath our feet let out a good snap
when crushed. He thrust his hand into mine and
I stepped out of his truck. Mistakes were made.
We might have gone on a walk. Jet planes tilted.

Could you see me splayed beneath him, under that
autumn sky, planes stuffed with peeping Toms? *Hail
Maryfullofgrace* in circles, on a loop, perpetual mono-
logue behind my teeth after he forced me to open up.

My habit worn in times of stress. He needed to bury his
beaten heart inside me. I needed to walk across the water
there at the end of my booted foot, where my jeans hugged
only one slim ankle. After that first time, I hid from green

Fords. But he always found me. We were *in love* he said
all through winter and spring and summer and the fall
that came with its letters of acceptance. Unwrapped
I left for school, where he posed as a sentinel outside

every one of my classes. Professor Heaney whispered
news of a better life inside an ivory tower. In no time
that learn'ed man's knuckles knocked upside my cheek
bone. I resisted his love laid bare by entering him first

with the blade of my knife. It was a statement my blue
eyed Irishman could not debate. I had learned to learn from
what others regret. I live now
with my last love. Years of trial and error. This man is equal

to my densely packed curriculum vitae. Son of an extreme
feminist, he knows subtlety, intimately. He will not hit me
over the head or pull my hair or make me carry the heavy
burdens. He hobbles me with the black and blue bouquets

that sprout beneath my dark roots. Now I know only this:
I would not like me, if I met my pink carnation eyes.

Tufted Titmouse with Its Funky Haircut

You are at home in a mob
attracted by others calling
you out. Your PETER-PETER-PETER
a song any slight bird can sing.
No ascending trill gone unmatched

just the usual birds. Yours is a beer
song, an all-occasion, feather-
my-nest with any quicksilver thing:
some hungover chick's discarded
pulltab plucked from high grass.

Black hair long enough to spiral
your nest's walls. The object
of her undoing, your bright spot
amid long days of sophomore girls
who hear only their own shame

in the song you sing at dawn. Used
up notes repeated ad nauseum.
They say you are common, a tit-
mouse, a comely bird in search
of anonymity in an unruly crowd.

A Circus Life

Skinny circus girl is braided through
with the sight and smell of it: peanuts
popcorn and burnt butter. The Fat Lady
breathes fire and Dog Boy was last seen
jumping through hoops, hopping mad
to hump a left leg and then the right, right
on up a crooked alley. Skinny gets high
on her flying trapeze but aims for the dirt
far beyond the Big Top's hoop skirt.

She will abide your hankering, thoughtless
wish to join the circus. Your dream deposits
her heart in a back pocket like the penny candy,
sawdust floors and freaks you don't see
when the tent's flap is zipped: the Ringmaster
mastering the ring, clowns tripping out
in the bed of a truck. Yet at every truck stop's
cracked sink she will rub her finger across her
teeth. Spit and eat. Sleep while towns full of kids
sleeping go skip-skidding past the windshield
wiper's bare blades. Drift and drift, always
ready to throw up some grommeted canvas
in lots left vacant beside identical highways.

Elle veut être française, not to be
the one who twirls beneath the point,
so she swallows her words scratched
in dust, when Lion roars she says *shhh*—

Nine's the Devil His Own Self

One for sorrow, two's mirth…,
And nine's the devil his ane sel'.

He's a grown man when he gets carried away
from the bathtub filled with blood. Transported
through warm water onto a stretcher, arms angled
in, he is wrapped. His brain jumps its track, skews
from this wound to old wounds brought to life
by the shrieking light. Synapse branch into hemlock

trees viewed from an upper window, and early snow
shushing six, seven, eight magpies. He was nine
the day his mother took flight. His brother turned away
or acted like he did, speaking idly of probability until
they went back to school. Walking beneath the weight
of so many leaves not yet fallen, these two disappeared

into other children. They fanned their hands wide, high
fived classmates. Kicked the can and later just the one
boy turned it 'round, felt his way into it: thin armor
for a beaten heart. This Tin Man, undaunted by missing
parts, wielded his pipe like an axe. Whistling a flat tune
he truncated all his thoughts before they grew.

Visits to Sing-Sing

Domestic etiquette is the weapon we
exploit. We speak of the heat, not her,

laid out and left on the Mediterranean
tile of our kitchen floor. His smile hits

me first as he grabs my hand, shaking it
while her eyes tug at me from inside

his cocked head. She is the undertow
this murdered woman who waves from

within my brother. The prison cutting
garden is his atonement. Here he severs

sunflower heads for their seeds. Visiting
day I cleave to him. Stretching my neck

across the plank table, I lean into his world
where he offers me a light.

To You, My Heart

It's you my heart, pounding silence, keeping
me awake. Sometimes the skin in its array of
colors strings me along. Often the descending
colon offers a jolt, unfamiliar twinge turning

me inside out. Almost never the pharynx, peri-
cardium, or the little heard from thymus. Four
humors now denied, since we made progress.
Do blood, bile, and phlegm ever really end?

Now we're pre-menstrual, bi-polar, depressed,
incontinent. Impotent against the bodily trauma
I trace with symptomatic mapping of ills like
worry beads on days when the vessel is empty.

Never in younger days did the machine do more
than function as it should. Careless careening
toward my ultimate outcome. Cholesterol
that hard gall of ancient Greece. Fats linger

in the mind to briefly torture, when mirrored
by a new suit's reflection of the me others will
view beside some long gone boy's pool house.
And still, as then, it's you my heart, cheating my

organs into taking the blame for all your ills and
aches. For the pain of you existing outside of you
ready to rest inside the vessel of anyone else.

Jacob's Ladder

Is this place where angels climb,
stepping up then down each day,
mere recreation or imitation?

Is there division in each step
in that *nothing but air* space
in between? We take one flight

up one ladder, rung by rung
with no rails and no grip, we
soon slip in the   between.

Artists call it negative space
while writers hear a breath
between words we choose

to signify how we climb
the Jesus bones aligned.
Are we reborn in the midst

of the slip   *whoosh*
where words are taken away
by what can't be

said or is it the strike of each
morpheme? Struct as the root
embodiment of build, construct

a solid structure, build a life
sentence in the syntax
of double negative spaces

damning us to the ladder, where
we choke on words spit like seeds
and on the fruit we hold back.

Rooting Ever Upward

Under weeds, plucked full-fisted,
her hand trembles at the root. Rooting
as in infant mouthing skin for milk.
Rooted as in buried at the base seeking
to find the once green cell to shoot up
and grow to shout with riotous violets
popped from stems to stretch toward
                    the never-ending blue.

Under water, in the deepest places,
darkness does not cancel the pressure
to wave and reach in unruly shocks
of twilight flora. The first life forms
again and again, feeding those who
have reached the light and rooted.

I came to you from the dirt, reaching
ever upward, full-fisted and flowering.

Part 2:

Lemoning Up

Riding the Pretty Horse

It's the hotpack for a heartbeat that won't sing. The sting
comesandcrams skid row dreams bawling up under her
skin. Left l o n g at the bottom there was no telling
the who or where of what went deadly dark departed

into her blazing summer days. She e v e r y d a y stands
too still and the stillness steals her breath
like that mad cat with his toothy grin. Soon she will begin,
held up or strung up, swaying in the tide, she opens wide

to testify at the height of her drop off the edge of e n d l e s s
silence. The white queen on the black square stares long
before fluxing the rx the cure the fluff built from bamboo
shoved up under manicured nails. Float the wet

desire, l i m p i d lids draw her in-
visible on a blank canvas. She grows darker than the days
of pink sunsets: always dressed for tea but longing
for dirt. The quick fix happy pop of hot dark tar beneath
her toes or, on cryptic days, her tongue.

On Banking

When life rises like water
      over the embankment built
for the reasons we all build

I check my bank account
clutch the cents left over
      after paying the bill. Mine

is a method meant to soothe
yet it nickels and dimes me.
      I start again

and count *me too*. One blue
fisted bulb beats its rhythm.
      Two pale breasts softly sit

atop twelve bones aligned
      to protect a single heart.

Then there's all the rest of this
body that won't stop. My hands
palmed in prayer
      when I can't lie
wrapped in the arms he drapes
across my hips for even one
      goodnight.

So I begin to count
      his words
and the bones   of sheep.

When the water rises
      above the bank
I practice a new stroke.

Desiring Goddesses

Do not dismiss their desire or consider it
                your own. It's not the same
heady atmosphere of wants satisfied.
                         Fancies met
turn trivial soon after. You imagine her
body is yours to gild. Your vision of her
never includes her

                        pulling white bread
from an oven. Aphrodite or Angelina. Act
Two: the back of her hand wipes sweat
from creamy skin   she is bent over
                  a hot stove.

On the silver screen or in a seashell
                  no goddess exists
before the maiden. Innocence bursts its pod
quick   as a seed plucked
from a pomegranate for the taste of tart red.

Place her at the fourth station of the cross.

Named for all the good girls the mothers
                stigmatized
                by their rise
from obscurity into pale blue beauty.
Neither deity nor plebeian   each lives
within   your denial of her.

Lost Luggage

Drop your bags. Let them become
lost, lifted, loosely held. No value
in what is packed for the weather
no one can predict. Fear lies flat

'til it is pulled up like a crumpled sheet
to cover a cool *Me, too.* You coil yourself
in that timeworn gesture of stained cloth
turned to shame. It exists in the women

you envy as they de-plane and glide down
the gate's plank, only to enter the great state
of panic. Frantic beside the turning carousel
deep inside every cavernous airport, each

begins circling, cycling through
                          all that was lost.
Not just leather, but Gucci-stamped leather
and slacks that only yesterday showed her
                          good side. Today

in new trousers, she will crease her brow
                          aim to view her back-
side at that one angle to catch a glimpse of how

these particular pants hang in the wrong place.
There are earrings, too, and panties, high-cost
                          creams, and a love letter.
The detailed losses mount her just the way he did

the last time. That time won't count. It was three
on a Thursday in another country. It is still
Thursday, not yet three but certainly the hour
for cocktails   somewhere.

Games

Turning fifty-one is like a game
of hide & seek, and she's run out
of do-overs. She chased down

every bubble, real or imagined,
jumped the broom times two. Hope
is a feather boa and tales of *I will
wear my hair long*, let it flow down

the castle wall, so the knight will come
and climb, hand-over-hand, breaking
the rope climb record he set long ago.

Last birthday, she cut her hair short
        dyed it bright red right after
he rounded all the bases and ran
off. Now she knows she knows

nothing but all the words forced
to fit the up and down rows of her
time worn Scrabble board.

Junkies in Late June

One at a time, some in pairs,
they reach for the other side

of the fence. They are tender
like sugar snap peas dangling

from their stems. One drops
to his knees in the dirt and

his woman tends him, swipes
her palm across his temple,

sweeps ashes from his scarred
collarbone and flicks away the

filter that hangs from his bruised
lips. This lean woman's fallen man

has just about lost his head in a nod.
Yet, she still has the sense to assess

each pedestrian as we pass through
their scattered rows. We share nothing

just a desire to be tender in late June.

Jane Flirts with Tragedy

The crazy lady in my attic hides
chin up, peering out from above
starched shirts. Tied in knots, she
mirrors Bertha's smile tacked on
by her silver bullet—*Revlon Red.*

I hear her sing, and I continue to
rinse each dish with care, longing
to join my voice. To her I am divine
comedy, lemoning drains for a fresh
scent.   She counts days passed

by cutting crosses into her patch
of dust. I count them by averting
my eyes. Twenty-eight days pass
                    without a blink.

Pericardium

Connected, I create a swell for you
from the ache that breaks your beat.
I cradle you to keep the oblique
harmony you set. And though it's true
we are not known as separate sweets
my candy coat is a cover for this beat
you you, you you, the body listens to.

My role is to serve. I know. Yet I build
from the body's sorrow a shallow river
to cushion your chambers. Her deriguere
fall too often fills you with songs to still
your rhythm. She sets her watch to regret
you follow in time, and I, too, am beset
with your pulsing fist as the beat I protect.

Were We Right to Choose?

Your hand held violets you wanted
to give me, after you took one
ripe bloom. The seed was planted
with care. You were all in then

but not when you said the flowers
were *forgotten in the 'fridge,* not
when I cried out   at the violence
done behind the doctor's door.

Before we knew it, we'd put it all
on ice. *Let it go,* you said. The final
word left me marooned while words
unsaid tattooed our grieving, gone

soft spots. Now you appear here
where serendipity placed you
                    next to me
on the aisle
                    and you want to

talk of your new wife, of her blight
of dropped blossoms, your adopted
child, who will not grow
                    and I want

to lay my head on that long-ago
kitchen table, think again, speak
                    to you prayers
of life as it slips through our hands.

My Life in Pajamas

To lounge or not to lounge: that is the question:
Whether 'tis nobler in the house to enjoy
The silks & flannels of domestic fortune,
Or to dress up against the tide of lassitude,
And by opposing choose Eros? Tie dye: to sleep;
No more; and by a slip to say we live
The heartbreak of the thousand thread-count sheets
That flesh wants next to, 'tis that consummation
Devoutly to be wish'd. To buy, for sleep;
To sleep? Perchance to dream: ay, there's the rub;
For in that daze of babes what sleep may come
When we have ruffled all the fine feathers down,
Must give us rest? There's the connect
That makes mockery of such short sleep;
For who would bear the pains and scars of birth,
The oppressed breast, that proud mom's superbity,
The pangs of des'prate love, the spouse delayed,
The near silence of Erato and the spurns
That patient husband of the sleepless takes,
When he himself might his reverie make
With a spare Ambien? Who would bundles bear,
To wipe and clean under a teary child,
But that the dread of no heir after death,
The undisclos'd revelry from whose life
No prodigy proclaims, quiets the mom
And makes her rather love those ills she has
Than fly to locales where Prada reigns.
Thus Hera does make fam'ly of us all;
And thus the pallid hue of exhaustion
Is covered o'er with the gold glow of Eos,
And strategies of great sheets do fail

To wit: regard the son who sleeps sweetly,
And lose the name of Hypnos. —Soft you now!
The fair Erato! Muse, in thy petition
Be all my dark circles forgott'n.

For Poetry

We learn to kill our darlings like Medea
        in love. We rip their bodies

formed from our breasts and mind not
        the mineral red that will follow

or the loss. Hemingway knew
        weapons matter, words fall

like embryos out of rhythm. They
        collide, cutting off thoughts

of other words, better words. Malformed
        utterances clamor to live. Once

unsheathed, the blade lifts this gate, while
        another closes, leaving only
                the ones we have left.

Nothing but Laundry

Oh, let there be nothing on earth but laundry
Nothing but rosy hands in the rising steam
And clear dances done in the sight of heaven.
　　　　　　　　　　—Richard Wilbur

The ruddy hands are hers, reaching out
to pull taut the corded rope cut to fit
the oak's girth, where her skirts tangle
with his slacks, rising and waving

on a chill wind. Her hips bones press
against their windowsill, she hangs
hard-wrung laundry on the line, her mind
moves and stays in place like a leaf eddying:

her silent prayers a dark habit. Turning
in to meet her husband's hands
gently pulling her to kneel before him
on clean sheets, she considers this

one more job to cross off today's list.
And just as quickly kneels again to run
a worn rag across the pine floor, reaching
into corners to polish even the plank

that broke. Skipping vespers she steps out
onto the brittle lawn and rests
a chair beneath the tree. Her sleight spirit hangs
a moment above the body that will not
wave back at the laundry, ready to be taken in.

Queen Holle

This frigid noon is crackle dry, not
quite tundra, up here at the top
of nowhere. A sepulchral tower of white
spun sugar. The sharp white of absolute
limits. I long for the fade, the slip

off today into a black that does not hold
any hope of hue or presence. No reason
to dress in slacks no longer slack or even
a dress meant to keep me in good
standing. Winter comes over me
like a bleached sack.

Washing Fruit

Washing fruit in lemon water defines her
arthritic fingers curved to close 'round
each apple. Untouched for years, she did
not pray for solace or   salvation

from her kitchen sink. Then she brooded
on baby baths, a teen's long line of cups,
and the daily nurture of a man who forgot
her name.   The woman

created by their need is a vision reflected
in bleached porcelain. While a young bride,
she was left wanting to run to a foreign place
a place with dishwashers and no list of chores

left undone. Today, her hands come together
grateful for the ritual of water thick with soap.

Who Knew You Loved

Plants. Who knew you loved

the pointed green ficus you left

behind? Daily it leafs its way

to me, angling into my bed.

I reach out to stroke its

long leaves. Some days I sing

like a songbird, nesting under

its branches. Me? I can't see

how the ficus won allegiance

above your family, the babies,

grandchildren you refused

to meet. There sits the Buddha

plant you haven't bothered to

mention in the list of property

worth much more in retrospect.

Still, we grow. These houseplants

and I hold secrets like presence

in the morning light, emptiness

at noon, belief in the pressure

that transforms water into life.

Interlude: Claridge's London

The public space tempts her
out of their made-up room.

She sits amid luxury, swirling
a good red, testing the edge.

Bespoke men appear busy: tap
tap, tap tapping at their laps–

she fingers her solitaire, recalls
the rush of lust. To raise the stakes,

she crosses her legs and enjoys the slip
as her skirt slides up. She strokes the

supple fabric and (almost absentmindedly)
lets one exquisite shoe dangle: a motion

like any other, yet a current
of undress under the chandelier.

All lit up, she eyes each man's rise
out of his laptop world. They glance

her way and she waits. A waiter
comes to her table, delivers her

a second glass and nods toward
the one man she missed.

Bones Don't Lie

I dreamed of you again last night. You ran
your finger one breath above my ankle bone.

In a room noisy with children, *yours and mine*
with our distracted spouses, we lingered.

No divorce, no defined line crossed. Only one
tantalizing finger floated. In a room, noisy

with children I stare, while a woman turns
her back. Her shoulders curve to create a cave

where her attention is devoured by the phone
she cradles. Kids lose patience and pin-the-tail.

His Hands

That he will never say goodbye reminds me of
small wadded pieces of paper he chose to keep

in hand: in his pockets, receipts, blank post-its
and scrawled notes on napkins even he could not

decipher. Sometimes he lay sleeping, a paper towel
crumpled in his fist. Curved in, his hands unused

to opening, they stay at his side even now—
their pale, smooth surface protected from me taking

my leave. His left hand with its wormpath scar circling
its newly naked finger is the only tell in this silent letting

go. He folds his hands as though anxious to place them
on a high shelf or perhaps in a scented drawer.

A Measure of Worth

The first technician turns my head
away. *Don't move.* She says after

divining the perfect position: forced
forward, crushed between steel plates

my flesh curdles.

Each consecutive tech lets me down
easy with tales of survival and pin-

curled pink ribbon. Enter three green
and sterile surgeons, each with his own

gift, *everyday* procedures

they concur, while their cutting fingers
twitch like Quintianus in love. Nearby

a cathedral's noon bells peal, startle me
with echoes of St. Agatha's ecstatic misery.

I want to die intact.

Doctor Barber preys on both breasts: *get*
all the cells gone wild. Mountebank wants

to *rebuild—bigger, firmer,* while Caduceus
speaks of caution, seeking to cut off

just the one—for now.

What Is Left

Pencils shaved to point and
                     then the shavings
apples peeled down to flesh
                     and the peelings,
hair brushed a hundred strokes
                     then the remains
old red grapes crushed and then
                     the marc left
babes birthed in faith and
                     then the leaving
mothers stroked until the skin
                     rises to one touch
nipples habituated and then the milk
                     heart's fist planted
and the bloody pail.

Part 3:

Kneeling Under the Lemon Tree

Kneeling Under the Lemon Tree

Sod rises up to meet my knees.
I lift my chin, and the juice
sours my skin. Give me some

sugar, and you know I will want
to make it up for you to sip slow
undo the acid. Reflexively

I rise to wake and squeeze thick
waxy lemons into the cure. I believe
in long-gone ways, quiet now and

likely lost. We once knew the way
to keep you. Mamas spoke the how
and when of mash and blend, taking
in the sweet with the sour.

A Single Black-Eyed Susan

Your trusting body bends low as
you garden up the lawn he cuts

some Saturdays before he breaks
for lemonade. On the hill, divided

from an always you and he share,
her mind is atilt in knowing you

don't know. There is a spin in this
two-step learned too late. First he

stared. And like those lemon days
she dropped, looked away. Single

as a Black-eyed Susan swaying
in your bed of daisies, her mouth

fronts a new body just out of reach.
Isn't that the balm that draws birds

and bees? His slow smile turned up
then spread until it covered her with

its sting. She became a skip in the record
you won't play, yet. She sweetened his

lemonade, saw dandelions not weeds. She
lifted off. He lifted her. He spoke of other

songs. She thought *protect the bulb,* don't
flower outside this careless cottage planted

on its hill. There is a beast in every garden.
There is a crackling hearth keeps his home

aglow. *There's an oven.* Over the hill
is forever. On this hill, he grows a fairytale
girl, who stoops to gather lost things in her

pretty pocket. Her pale hands hide folded
bits of a language no one will ever hear.

Home Repair

You are workin' it all night
constructing myth with your
your calloused hands. Or is it
the currency of your thick lips
through which a slow smile
speaks, when your beaten heart
sings a black currant jam
between my teeth. And then
you ache me invisible. I am
the toast and you the spread
up under my skin. You tell it
like it isn't. Then say, *okay
why you mad?*

One Stitch Too Many

Words like mama's threaded needle puncture
me. Up, down, in, out, and again. He twists
the blues in with threads of yellow like that
wallpaper peeling off walls in Charlotte's tale
about losing. My mind bends beneath remains

of gestures. Our talks all tilt-a-wheel tactics
to keep me petaling, even now he comes behind
me, his hands reaching for my hips. His word
has no meaning in a world of words spit only
to corner me. He eases into the turn

asks me to stop thinking. Instead I open
his sent mail and read how he speaks of me
to her, the one he said moved on. I'm meant
to say *I'm sorry,* cook something good, stumble
to bed, whispering *I lay me down to sleep.*

Collected to Be Returned

His hands are busy with returning
bottles lifted from his immaculate
Mercedes. His eyes are lifted too—
brown and amber, sparkling as they
capture her in passing. She becomes

aware of his gaze out there at that
intersection of downtown and uphill
after thirty days of running in a gym
next to him climbing stairs. His brown
eyes lifting her to his lips, taking her in

his mind, muddy with want. An always
story of spark and start, not the always
tale of middle of the road marriage, here
all the lights turn green, but do not mistake
this always for *endless*. These are all the ways

of returning emptied, a lover's hands held
out, lifted, waiting for the change to drop.

More Than What You Came For

Can my watchful eyes turn from
green to liquid blue? You know
the accepting gaze of clear skies
witless wonder in the simple sex
of orgasm. Can my lips open to
you and never speak what came
before or what comes now? Unsay
what was said, unthink cause and
effect?
                    Wedded
to this precipice and the fall, can we
                    undo the knot
you tied or the others slipped deftly
                    over my blue
wrists? Can you unportion each dish
                    unserved?
This is the sex of swallowing
crumbs. The girl you grew up
wanting to reject. Comely doll
your small sisters accepted as their
only gift, their undoing. A Barbie
in cotton shifts, hair unlike, eyes un-
open, skin unbrown, under a G.I Joe.

Can you reverse your gaze? Can you
undo your desire in what is not
yours to undress and redress
the image you conjured, fill it in
with more than what you came for?

This Is Not a Love Song

I drag down one last cigarette, one last
cigarette, one last time, inspired to quit
even as the smoke fills the spaces around
the space you leave, when you leave me

filled and breathless. I stack clean sheets
layer them, then I go on to layer clean
cups, saucers or plates, fill cabinets
you didn't choose with clean dishes

in patterns you will never see. Sweet
shards of ceramic bloody my feet
                           after I drop to the floor
that coffee cup you used. I neatly stack

the pieces in a pile, erect a cairn to top
this grave we are digging. Is there room
in there for two? This body and that one,
yours, contain a flint and a stone. A basic

chemistry set, unwrapped like a Christmas
gift, a small holiday, slight vacation, present
with no past or unfurling days to plan
farther down the road. When you are gone

hours later, I count my days in minutes
and stack them, too. All just magic tricks
my fingers play with my mind.

How to Confess

—after William Carlos Williams

This is just to say you can't
forgive me.

That is to say you will
never know.

This is just to say telling you
is a lie to save you.

That is my tongue unfurling
content as a fat pussycat's.

This is just to say you know
everything.

That is to say you have it all
and may taste it, too.

This is just to say that story's
been told.

That is to say the untelling
is the story I am telling.

This is just to say I have licked
my need to confess.

Fairytale

Heat wave and a stranger. Always
the cool stranger, who speaks you
into being what he thinks he sees

when he blocks your crumbling
path. There you become fairytale
pretty, perfect-bound, bound and

shut mouth. He carries handcuffs
and a government issued gun
as a matter of course. You forget

red hood (*hide*), red apple (*cyanide*),
red lips (*guide*), apropos of nowhere
new to go on a hot day. A diner

on her way into the Castle Cafe.
A click seals your cliché fall, no
sirens blair, no wrote down laws

broke. Fairy tales reveal ogres
to their readers right quick but
never to the desired, until it's—

He's fittin' to strip slight bits
of you. The tissue connecting
your soul to your cross. Fallen

you rewrite your tale in spun sugar
bridges built on solid ground. You
genuflect and make him reel. There

is also and always a Mama he turns
to. Hers is a deep well we all best
drink from, for mamas rise as girls fall.

Grimm

Shove her into those crystal
shoes. Bound, she might
writhe or hiss. Salty words
forced from prim lips. Kiss

each verruca as it rises. Bend
her to your version of the un-
spoken fairytale. Work your
way from her silken feet on up.

Unhinge her hips like a snake's
maw. She will bear your hard
press, if only for her chance
to braid a girl's spiraled hair

and escape down its strands
knotted painstakingly. Cling
round her breast at night then
rise in time to see her milk

curdle. She will never conceive
of your terms. Her lips appled
into only a reflection of you.

Blind

*Oooh I would rather, I would rather go
blind boy.* Etta opens her throat to let

her man hear her sing. Her presence
once endowed by the gods with every

good thing, returned to her as a curse.
His honey, meager and warm, pours

from that hole to cover her one lie

at a time. Now bound in a bottle, a jar
or a mythical box, each syllable a note

like Sylvia's slight of tongue, cut *off
at the root.* Etta sings the blues. Boy

every good thing ain't worth seeing—
if I have to watch you walk away.

Undoing What We Know

Forgive me Our Father; forgive my father
his sin in having me, giving up on the one

he loved in sins shared, squared, round
it off. Child of sin, bastard, sordid bitch

is what he let in; what she took in; what
fell from above and got dragged to mud.

The Godhead. His word, and the voices
of you and she; me in full flight from we.

Birthed into a beaten heart and bled, four-
square, hopscotch, doubledutch. Now my

man breaks the faith, enters caves, rolls
his tongue around my words and ways to

broom the jump. This here one constructs
a temple to deconstruct. *Do it.* Blood let us

go and undo all we know. Know I won't
look back. I'd never be your pillar of salt.

Blood and Bone

When morning comes
                like this one did
enfolded in the last night's
precedence, dead set
against bearing
                the weight of one
end-stopped and alone,
she rises reassembled.

Only pretty parts came
                unbruised.
Lifted into his hands
she is seen. Her skin
knits the stones of
                her single story
into ghost chains of DNA
aligned to gift him a
                grafting of her
petaled blood to his bone.

An Act of God

You came to me with your breath. Breathing me
in, you lingered just outside the open door. *Come
inside.* I invited you in, measured the degree of
care required, cooked ribs and fed you, then ate

an apple, made apple pies, biscuits and picked up
crumbs. I stripped off your clothes, threw them
in the machine at midnight. Pleased you like I was
buying a policy to offset catastrophic loss. You

brought your broad shoulders to fix what you saw
needed fixing. You assessed the risk. You gave
assurances. A grace period. I was unaware I had
provided a free-look provision, so I continued

to wonder where you were, when you were not
present. Having recently learned probability
I saw a deck stacked against success. Natural
and probable consequences of mortality tables

triggered negative trends no amount of risk
based capital can cover. Our policy will have
to be renewed with no insurance required.

Running

Watching you run. Your legs
licked with long muscles. There
is you and just beyond you

a trinity of windows faces the distant
horizon, constant, unresolved. You run
in the one place I come without pride

or vanity, and you become the object
in the distance. I remain invisible
like the pane you stride toward. Long

minutes torn into seconds. I run through
all the reasons I should stop but your skin
quickens me. People and their faces fall

away. You run. I run. Your sweat
courses the slippery length of you
and I clock its circuit. Your body

a vessel for my pull and release, dash
and drag footfall, my blood's new pace.
This rush is my opiate. No wasted energy

for memory imitating a stitched rib. No
thought enters this space between you
running and me running only to watch
you run—

On the Road

Blacktop, rock salt, sand or pebbles, under my feet
the hard press as I run or lie, after, on my pillow-top
mattress. I could not abide even one green snap pea
up under my sole. And then I

                         can. *I think I can.* I no
longer no, yes or maybe
                       my way through. I do.

I do and weather not the rain or blame
tears or tearing in my shin. I run like
you said I could. Tiara white, dress yellow   I do
run into you and the arms
                    of God. I sing like you

taught me. I reach out, fill my palms with the sense
of five fingers breezed by leaves and the leaving
that hardened me into cloud billow over daffodil.
                 Royal
                 blue princess
                        brought up
to speed, turned to lavender queen, who sees the spoils
of ripe fruit fallen to seed new paths that bloom fast into
                 orchards of what will be.

She Used to Play Dress-Up in the Daisies

She climbed through a window even though
          you left
               the door open.
You stood up straight. And then you fed her
words from your bare hand. She never bit
you but climbed through another window

to peer at you from the curb. You left her
there once or twice and hollered   *loser*
loser then *winner winner chicken dinner!*

You stood up straighter, whispered the code
for all the doors   you kept locked.
She came right up to your front door without

a code. She climbed into every opening.
You began to lock the windows and leave
a side door ajar, a crack, a sliver

inviting her to stay inside. She played
Thumbelina, slipped inside to soothe
the swallow broken beneath your ribs.

You built your house long ago with nuts
and bolts, a hammer and plain white glue.
She played house most of her life. Ran

with scissors, sat on counter-tops, left
her bed unmade; she stole lilacs, sweetly
balancing on a fence, and she spent years

without flowers. One bright day broke her
will, so she buried your swallow beneath
a field of narcissus, and walked away.

The Deconstruction of L-o-v-e
(or Meaning Deferred)

I ride the rails of your long, long, longer than days
away spent missing you legs that stretch out to
parenthetically possess me. You are my cadence,
my syntax, the grammar that makes me think *I*

just now began to think. I won't *think again,* won't
hesitate at the comma of my stutter-stopped heart.
My stifled cries build a soliloquy to the silent
space, where breath becomes a quiet that creates

how we mean. Upright but sans serif, you are there
in the curve of your name. I want to speak it out loud,
in whispers, in a crowd. You must speak my short story,
punctuate it, make it your own, give your name to it

written here in black and white, while you grow behind
my teeth. My lips cover the scars marking the places
that speak to me your history. Pain overcome, speaking
in tongues, a new language snakes across our blank page.

Ascension

Mountains capped in sheer blue
and the spring that always flows
giving small things far below
time to blossom petal white

and bright. The center of life
is a sweet spot of yellow. You
and the mountain stir visions
of ascension. That carved up-

sweep fills me with only one
desire: Climb. Hand-over-hand
like combat, until my shoulders
strain, and my core becomes

centered by the breath of daisies.
One stem in a wave of green
face open to the mountain and
beyond to the sun in its place.

Rooted there at the base in black
dirt. That will be my resting place.
In the sweet spot, yellow and still,
I choose reverence. Mountain and

You—visions of absolute peaks not
meant to be navigated. Ascension
is the work of a lifetime on one's
knees, while the path changes with

each day's shift. Tethered to one side,
cantilevered over cliffs in the embrace
of a blue so stunning I saw stars when
what sustains me is the meadow.

Never This

Never this twist
up
rooted tree.

Never this rope
slung
over a branch.

Never this not
knowing
what he did.

Never this un
doing
petal peel.

Never this turn
down
into dirt.

Never this clank
clicked
'round my wrists.

Never this room's
three
plastic chairs.

Never this never
next
day cock's crow.

Finding the Groove

Bearing all his tricks handed over
like treats, down
              his long slide further
into himself, I plucked strings and
played music in my head. Each night
he came to bed more dead
              to me. Now
man by man I measure bones to adjust
the armature of my penance. Each man's
              eyes mere marbles tossed
into the ring with their frank stare. Serial
builder, I repeat my mistakes, building up
masked men in a suit of
              what's familiar
until one man rises from the choir. He
wields his ax and cuts
              a clean path that speaks
to me in the groove of gospel.

Entropy is Forever

Endurance is the archetype hearts
of runners protect. What keeps us
running is neither here nor there.

Flux is the two step in a river bed
whose colors are always running.

You placed a hand on my hip and
I fell into step like your *babygirl*
standing on your shoes to learn

the dance. Is me runnin' to be in line
with whatever you need, now, entropy?

There's a stereo and an old radio and
a type you like. A stereotype. You
project a me like I'm meant to be

on the silver screen. Images in quickstep
a rhythm unmatched by the electric

slide of who you are; forever turn't up,
you turn out to be/or not to be with me.
I am a slight projection of the image you

love to hate. China, porcelain, (tempered
glass?) doll you cannot love—Babyboo.

My eyelids flip open to take you in and
you can't relate, you retaliate, you hate

to love. To lose control is a flickering flame
of contempt and contentment. Fluctuate

is an action to which you are addicted.
you initiate the repetition of a rhythm.
The strong, black, male lead who can't

"c'mon get happy," because to do so
would require breaking the wall you don't

see, the one or three that hold you to be
playing a role in a counterfeit history. Entropy
is forever changing the heart of my story.

One Letter from Morning

The you is key to how
I get to *good morning*
on those dizzying days
when you sing me into
being. It's unbecoming

how swiftly the letter
fades. No postage need
stand squarely in my
top-right corner to get me
to you. You mark my words

tote the weight of my pulse
beating me to sleep with
your rise and fall, that breath
that says you'll envelope me
in every way, even when it's

sticky, and we risk a paper cut
lip. And then there's *this you.*
The one who wakes
to leave like long distance will
be the blue uniform to deliver

the letter. *This* you; the one who
changes good morning to plain
old post-it note reminders of the
everyday ways this love is just
one more letter into mourning.

I No Longer Know

I no longer know how to think

about who you are or why. I'm disabled
        by your consistently intermittent

disconnect. Long spiraling goldenrod
phone cords come to mind. *Why?*
Is my? Is your? Is the rooted tongue
kept clipped, so it won't spew words

or sing us to sleep? The phone phones
me up, so I can twist the cord and cradle

our connection. Doused in your musk, smoke
and my vanilla, in an old kitchen in my mind.
Can you tell? It's telling that you are able
bodied yet keep your limbs so still. A tell

me night, a Sunday, of cheap long distance
tales, of warm dough rising in a blue bowl,

all the ways this always ends in your kitchen.
When finally I pack my dishes, my panties left
for me, hanging in an unused bedroom. Hidden
I am cooking something good even though you

won't open your mouth. I swallowed all your
tomorrows. I buttered bread. Fresh from a hot

shower, I shifted your place at my table, moved
      myself closer to the oven. I want to hang up
but the cord's gone 'round my ankle, and it is
working its way up my throat. There isn't enough

space between me and this receiver I want to hang
up hard in its homely gold box. Remember when

someone said something you didn't like hearing?
You untwisted the cord, dangling it to unspin,
        to set it straight, and then you let it lie
on the cool tiles   while you wandered out

of the room, that kitchen, where all the talk
was left. You were right. It's not your words.

Fasching Days

...whether out of ignorance or a desire to portray Baldur as a martyr-like figure, Snorri likely omitted a key element of Baldur's character: a warlike disposition.

Dan McCoy—*Norse Mythology for Smart People.*

In the bath, between your legs, I lean into
the real you. I close my eyes and women
create a clamor inside my head. Known

as crazy days; snip a man's tie below the
knot, give him a festival kiss. Unknotting
in the bath, between your legs, I lean into

women cutting you loose. Fasching sounds
like fucking. I say, *sex like shaking hands?*
and create a clamor inside my head. Known

as my Baldur, your laugh fills this tub with
me again. Happily ever after raises its head
in the bath between your legs, so I lean into

our long minute. The whole world weeps red.
I should have named you Narcissus. Mirrors
create a clamor inside my head. Knowing

you have climbed, un tied, out of the nether
world's bed, I bring sugar. You salt my sea.
In the bath, between your legs, I lean into
creation's clamor inside my head. Knowing.

These Are Her Words

These are her words I sift like salt
through swollen lips. Prayers for
little girls turned to prey. *It's been
a minute since I fed you,* he said.

Her words are pearls cracked and
crumbling. His words I swallow
along with my own. But her words
I sift like salt for prayer. The known

testify on the far edge of the sea.
She sings songs of innocence, sirens
undone by shifting sands. His hands
rub me raw. His eyes have no word

for how he turned me sea glass soft
from oft' used, broken pieces of what
was once whole. I use her words,
iridescent grains of truth, sifted

like salt into prayer. He feeds me.
She feeds me what I cannot testify
standing on the sharp edge, closed
mouth, inside this sea shell made

to hold girls who grew too much
too fast too bright too shiny too
too soon. No bible passage words
it right. It starts in the eyes of others

long before we learn to dim our light.

Mathematics, God, & Seashells

He invited me in
to math this life
in a taut exchange
of deconstruction.

God showed up
in his eyes. I had to look
away or I might—

Uncertainty was on
the face of everyone
seated there that night.
The whorl of his finger-

print matched the swirl
of my skirt as our talk
turned to seashells and
Fibonacci. He is a light

squared and sent to shine
in the quiet corners of my
negative spaces. If my brain
is the observer, and not one

of this body's limits exist,
then two ones become two
minds in concert. We set out
to spin a single song.

To Fall

She fell and skinned her shin-
bone, ankle to knee but got up
to run. *To fall: to come or drop*
down suddenly to a lower position
whether voluntarily or not.

It's in the knot that falls into place
in the heart. It seems so vast
and varied *to fall: to drop one's*
eyes, to be directed downward.
The pratfall is about the only one

that brings a grin. Or falling, as we
once did, in love. There is gravity
in it. A grave mishap it may be to fall
for him. Lemons fall like bounty dropped
      ripe to the earth ready for some sugar.

About the Author

Michele Lesko's poems and short stories have appeared in various print and online journals. Her poem, "Interlude: Claridge's London," won a Reader's Choice Award at *Pedestal Magazine*. She is a graduate of Fairleigh Dickinson University and is the founding editor of *IthacaLit: Lit with Art,* an online poetry journal that features the annual $1,000 Lauren K. Alleyne Difficult Fruit Poetry Prize.

Kelsay Books

www.ingramcontent.com/pod-product-compliance
Lightning Source LLC
Chambersburg PA
CBHW031000090426
42737CB00007B/612